Start TO Finish
Second Series

Food

FROM Grass TO Milk

STACY TAUS-BOLSTAD

LERNER PUBLICATIONS COMPANY ▸ Minneapolis

Lerner Publications Company
A division of Lerner Publishing Group, Inc.
241 First Avenue North
Minneapolis, MN 55401 U.S.A.

For reading levels and more information, look up this title at www.lernerbooks.com.

Photo Acknowledgments
The images in this book are used with the permission of: © Anna Sedneva/Dreamstime.com, p. 1; © Todd Strand/Independent Picture Service, p. 3; Agricultural Research Service, USDA, pp. 5, 13, 21; © Aleksas Kvedoras/Dreamstime.com, p. 7; © Koki Iino/Getty Images, p. 9; © Graeme Norways/Stone/Getty Images, p. 11; © Trinity Muller/Independent Picture Service, p. 15, 17, 19; © TTH/a.collectionRF/Getty Images, p. 23.

Front cover: © Peter Cade/Iconica/Getty Images.

Main body text set in Arta Std Book 20/26.
Typeface provided by International Typeface Corp.

Library of Congress Cataloging-in-Publication Data

Taus-Bolstad, Stacy.
    From grass to milk / by Stacy Taus-Bolstad.
        p.   cm. — (Start to finish. Second series, food)
    Includes index.
    ISBN 978-0-7613-9179-1 (lib. bdg. : alk. paper)
    ISBN 978-1-4677-0108-2 (eBook)
    1. Dairying—Juvenile literature. 2. Dairy cattle—Juvenile literature. 3. Cows—Juvenile literature. 4. Milk—Juvenile literature. I. Title.
SF239.5T38 2013
636.2'142—dc23   2011036405

Manufactured in the United States of America
3 – PC – 10/1/13

TABLE OF Contents

Milk helps me grow. Where does it come from?

A cow eats grass.

Many people drink milk that comes from cows.
A cow starts to make milk when she is ready
to have a baby. The mother cow eats grass.
Grass helps her live, grow, and make milk.

The cow makes milk.

The milk is made in the cow's udder. The udder looks like a bag. It hangs down at the back of the cow's body.

A farmer milks the cow.

A farmer uses a milking machine to milk cows. The farmer places a cow's **teats** into the milking machine. The teats hang down from the udder. The machine pulls on the cow's teats.

Tanks cool the milk.

The milk flows from the cow's teats.
Then it goes through hoses into a
tank. The tank cools the milk.

Trucks take the milk.

A large truck comes to the farm. The milk is put into the truck's tank to keep it cool. The truck carries the milk to a factory.

Machines clean the milk.

The milk may be dirty from the cow's body. Workers at the factory put the milk into machines. The machines remove the dirt from the milk.

The milk is heated.

A machine heats the milk. Heating kills **germs** in the milk. Germs can make people sick. Then the milk is cooled. Workers test the milk to make sure it is safe to drink.

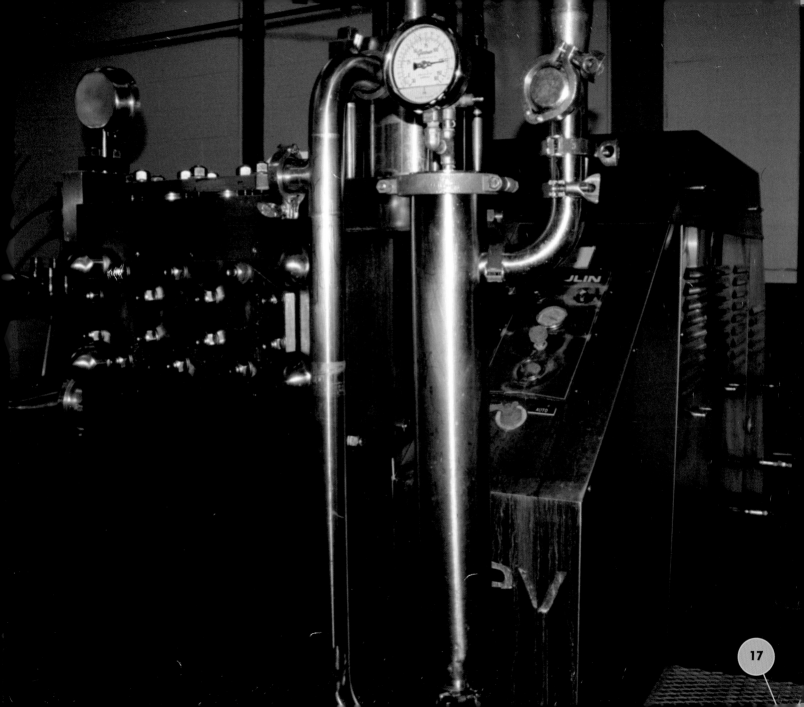

Machines put the milk in jugs.

The milk goes to another machine. This machine puts it into jugs. The jugs are sealed and put on trucks.

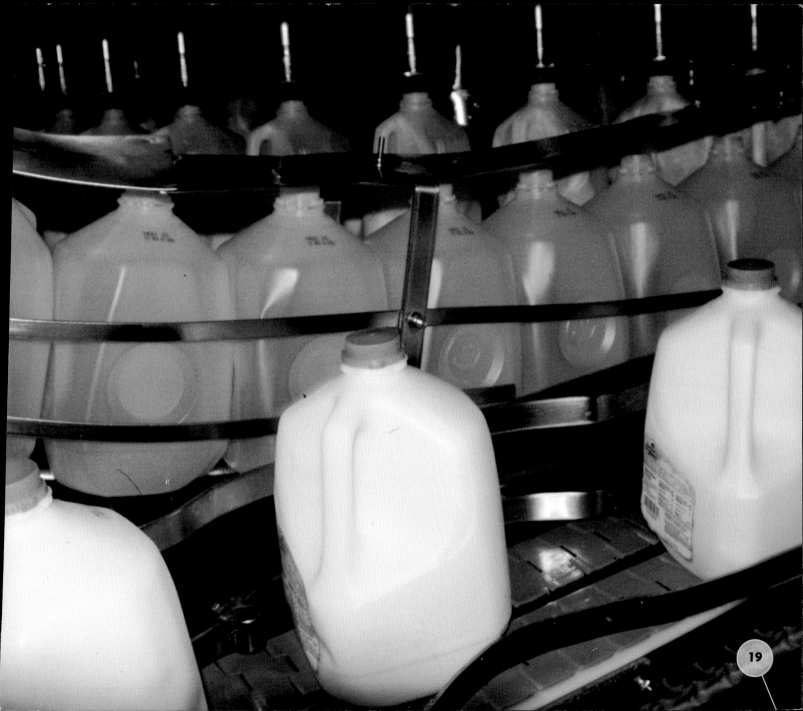

People buy the milk.

Trucks take the milk to stores. People buy the milk and take it home.

Yum! Cold milk.

Would you like a glass of cold milk? This tasty drink has gone from grass to milk.

Glossary

germs (JURMZ): tiny objects in milk that can cause sickness

teats (TEETS): the parts of a cow that milk flows out of

udder (UH-dur): the part of a cow that makes milk

Index

LERNER
e
SOURCE

Expand learning beyond the printed book. Download free, complementary educational resources for this book from our website, www.lerneresource.com.